Understanding the Human Body

BY
WENDI SILVANO

COPYRIGHT © 2009 Mark Twain Media, Inc.

ISBN 978-1-58037-486-6

Printing No. CD-404105

Mark Twain Media, Inc., Publishers
Distributed by Carson-Dellosa Publishing LLC

Visit us at www.carsondellosa.com

Table of Contents

Introduction

The human body is one of the most complex and fascinating organisms in existence. Having a basic understanding of how it functions is valuable knowledge. This book is designed to be a resource for teachers and parents to enhance and extend a textbook unit on the human body. It can be used as a tool to review already-covered concepts or even as a way to present new learning in a straightforward, simple way.

The units cover cells, tissues, organs, the major body systems (skeletal, muscular, circulatory, lymphatic, digestive, respiratory, excretory, nervous, and endocrine), as well as the five senses. Basic information is presented in a text format that is open and less dense than many texts. This makes it more readable and less intimidating for many students. Activities connected with the basic information provide opportunities for reviewing what has been presented.

Key terms appear in **boldface**. Many pages include **Far Out Facts**, which are fun tidbits of information that make the study of the human body even more fascinating. Also included are a number of **Webwise** websites that provide students the opportunity to further explore particular systems or concepts presented in the activities. Several of the websites relate to various body systems and are listed in each appropriate section.

A correlation to the National Science Education Standards is included on the next page.

Correlation to National Science Education Standards

This standards chart only includes those categories of the National Science Standards that apply to the materials in this book. (For example, Earth and Space Science Standards and Technology Standards did not apply, therefore they were left out.)

Standard	Activities (page numbers)
Unifying Concepts and Processes:	
Systems, order, and organization	7, 10, 12, 13, 14, 16, 18, 19, 21, 22, 23, 25, 26, 27, 29, 34, 35, 36, 37, 38, 39, 40, 41, 42, 44, 45, 46, 47, 48, 49, 50, 51, 52, 53, 54, 55, 56, 57, 58, 59, 60, 61, 62, 63, 64, 65, 66, 67, 68
Evidence, models, and explanation	7, 9, 10, 12, 13, 16, 18, 19, 20, 21, 23, 24, 25, 26, 27, 29, 31, 32, 33, 34, 35, 36, 37, 38, 39, 40, 41, 42, 43, 44, 45, 46, 47, 48, 49, 50, 51, 52, 53, 54, 55, 56, 57, 58, 59, 60, 61, 62, 63, 64, 65, 66, 67, 68, 69, 70, 71, 72, 73
Change, constancy, and measurement	14, 21, 22, 29, 33, 38, 41, 44, 46, 51, 52, 54, 59, 61
Evolution and equilibrium	14, 21, 29, 38, 39, 41, 43, 46, 49, 50, 61, 62, 63, 64, 65, 66, 67, 68
Form and function	7, 9, 10, 11, 12, 13, 14, 15, 16, 17, 18, 19, 20, 21, 22, 23, 24, 25, 26, 27, 28, 29, 30, 31, 32, 35, 36, 37, 38, 39, 40, 41, 42, 43, 45, 46, 47, 48, 49, 50, 51, 52, 53, 54, 55, 56, 57, 58, 59, 60, 61, 62, 63, 64, 65, 66, 67, 68, 69, 70, 71, 72, 73
Science as Inquiry Standards:	
Understanding about scientific inquiry	24, 52, 63, 73
Physical Science Standards:	
Properties and changes of properties in matter.	7, 9, 16, 18, 21, 23, 25, 33, 34, 38, 40, 41, 45, 46, 47, 48, 49, 50, 51, 52, 56, 57, 58, 59, 60, 61, 65, 70, 71, 73
Motions and forces	24, 25, 26, 27, 29, 30, 31, 32, 33, 34, 36, 37, 38, 39, 44, 45, 46, 47, 48, 49, 50, 51, 52, 53, 54, 55, 56, 57, 58, 59, 60
Transfer of energy	7, 24, 26, 27, 29, 30, 32, 34, 36, 38, 43, 44, 45, 46, 47, 48, 49, 50, 56, 61, 62, 63, 64, 65, 66, 69, 70

Correlation to National Science Education Standards (cont.)

Life Science Standards:	
Structure and function in living systems	7, 8, 9, 10, 11, 12, 13, 14, 15, 16, 17, 18, 19, 20, 21, 22, 23, 24, 25, 26, 27, 28, 29, 30, 31, 32, 33, 34, 35, 36, 37, 38, 40, 41, 42, 43, 44, 45, 46, 47, 48, 49, 50, 51, 52, 53, 54, 55, 56, 57, 58, 59, 60, 61, 62, 63, 64, 65, 66, 67, 68, 69, 70, 71, 72
Regulation and behavior	7, 8, 10, 25, 26, 29, 33, 34, 36, 41, 44, 51, 52, 53, 54, 55, 56, 57, 58, 59, 60, 61, 62, 63, 64, 65, 66, 67, 68, 74
Science in Personal and Social Perspectives:	
Personal health	10, 28, 33, 34, 35, 41, 42, 43, 61, 74

Cells: The Building Blocks Of Life

Far Out Fact: The average adult male has more than 100 trillion cells in his body.

Webwise: www.cellsalive.com

The human body is made of up of trillions of tiny parts called cells. There are all different types of cells within you. There are bone cells, blood cells, skin cells, heart cells ... and so forth. Cells don't all look alike, but all cells have some things in common.

Here are some main parts of a cell and what they do:

- **Cell membrane:** Acts sort of like a skin around the outside of the cell. It helps control which materials can go in and out of the cell. It lets oxygen and food in and waste products out. This helps maintain the chemical balance in and around the cell.

- **Nucleus:** Acts like the brain of the cell. It controls the cell's activities, just as your brain controls your body's activities. A thread-like hereditary material inside the nucleus called **chromatin** is made of protein and **DNA**. DNA is like a set of chemical instructions that tell the cell what to do.

- **Cytoplasm:** Gelatin-like substance inside the membrane containing water and chemicals.

- **Organelles:** Inside the cytoplasm are a variety of small structures sometimes called organelles. Each has a job in the cell.
    - *Endoplasmic Reticulum:* Moves material within the cell sort of like it was on conveyor belts. It is a folded membrane.
    - *Ribosomes:* Some are attached to the endoplasmic reticulum; others are just in the cytoplasm. They receive directions from the DNA to make proteins.
    - *Golgi Bodies:* Pack up the waste proteins to move them outside the cell.
    - *Mitochondria:* Uses food molecules to make and release energy.

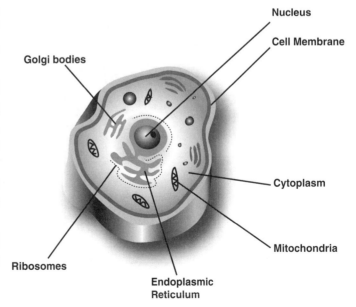

Name: _____ Date: _____

What's in a Cell?

Use the words from the word bank to name each part described below. Then use the names of the parts to label the drawing of a cell.

nucleus	cell membrane	cytoplasm	mitochondria
chromatin	Golgi bodies	ribosomes	endoplasmic reticulum

1. Gelatin-like substance where the work of the cell is done _____

2. Thread-like hereditary material made of DNA and proteins _____

3. Packages materials to take outside the cell _____

4. Cells make their proteins on these two-part structures. _____

5. Directs all the activities of the cell _____

6. Releases energy for the cell _____

7. Outer boundary of cell that controls what goes in and out of it _____

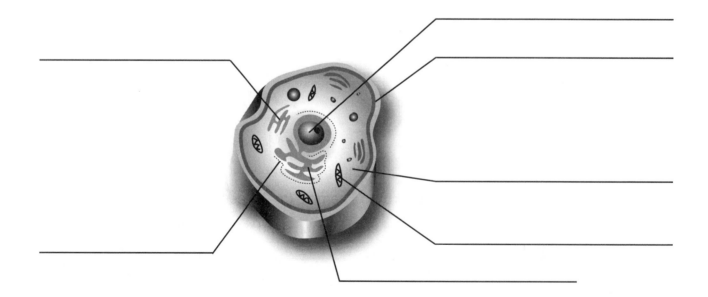

Name: _____ Date: _____

Tissue Types

Certain cells of the same type group together to form tissues. There are four basic types of tissues.

> **Far Out Fact:** Talk about epithelials! Much of the dust on our floors and furniture is actually dead skin cells that we shed by the millions every day!

Fill in the missing vowels in the incomplete words in the paragraphs below to review the four tissue types.

1. **C __ n n __ c t __ v __** tissue supports things and **h __ l d s** them **t __ g __ t h __ r.** You can find connective tissue **__ n d __ r** your **s k __ n** and in your **t __ n d __ n s.** Connective tissue is also what keeps your **__ r g __ n s** in place.

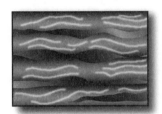

2. **__ p __ t h __ l __ __ __ l** tissue **p r __ t __ c t s** you by enclosing and **c __ v __ r __ n g** other parts of the body. These tissues make up your **s k __ n** and **l __ n e** the insides of your **m __ __ t h, t h r __ __ t,** and **d __ g __ s t __ v __** tract.

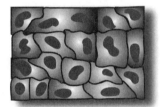

3. **M __ s c l __** tissue is made up of muscle **f __ b __ r s.** The three types of muscle tissue are **s k __ l __ t __ l, s m __ __ t h,** and **c __ r d __ __ __ c.** Skeletal muscles

m __ v __ the **b __ n __ s** and are **v __ l __ n t __ r y** muscles. Smooth muscles are **__ n v __ l __ n t __ r y** muscles and move many of your internal **__ r g __ n s.** Cardiac muscle is found only in the **h __ __ r t** and is also **__ n v __ l __ n t __ r y.**

4. **N __ r v __ __ s** tissue is found in the **b r __ __ __ n, s p __ n __ l c __ r d,** and the **n __ r v __ s.** It consists of cells called **n __ __ r __ n s.**

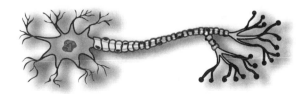

Name: _____ Date: _____

Mystery Organs

Far Out Fact: **The largest internal organ is the small intestine, which would stretch for 22 feet if removed from your body.**

Webwise: http://www.bbc.co.uk/science/humanbody/body/ (click on organs)

Organs are made of groups of more than one type of tissue. Each organ has a specific job to do within the body and often works in combination with other organs. Use the clues below to determine which organ is which.

1. I am part of the circulatory system.
   I have four chambers.
   Parts of me are the aorta and valves.
   What organ am I? _____

2. I am part of the digestive system.
   I secrete bile to help break down fats.
   I filter waste products from the blood.
   What organ am I? _____

3. I am the largest organ of the body.
   I protect your body and help regulate your temperature.
   One of my layers is the epidermis.
   What organ am I? _____

4. I am located in your lower back.
   I am part of the excretory and circulatory systems.
   I filter blood and remove fluids.
   What organ am I? _____

5. I am part of the endocrine and the digestive systems.
   I secrete digestive enzymes.
   I secrete the hormone insulin.
   What organ am I? _____

6. I take in oxygen and give off carbon dioxide.
   I am part of the respiratory system.
   I contain bronchioles and alveoli.
   What organ am I? _____

7. I am part of the nervous system.
   Some of my parts are the medulla, the cerebellum, and the cerebrum.
   I am filled with billions of neurons.
   What organ am I? _____

8. I am part of the digestive system.
   I am where nutrients from digested food are absorbed.
   My inner walls are lined with villi.
   What organ am I? _____

Name: _____ Date: _____

Scrambled Organs

Far Out Fact: If your tissues and organs don't get oxygen, your blood will turn blue.

An organ is a structure containing two or more different types of tissue that function together for a common purpose. See if you can unscramble the names of these organs of the human body from top to bottom.

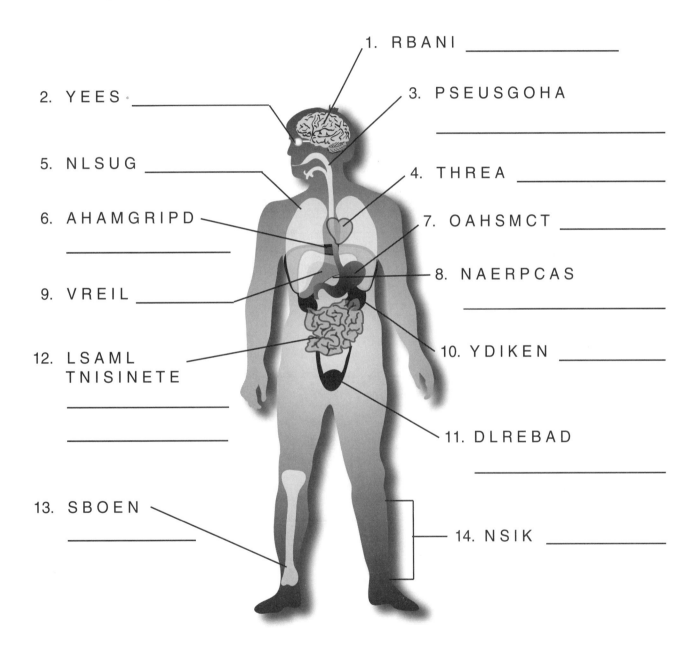

1. R B A N I _____

2. Y E E S _____

3. P S E U S G O H A _____

_____

5. N L S U G _____

4. T H R E A _____

6. A H A M G R I P D _____

7. O A H S M C T _____

9. V R E I L _____

8. N A E R P C A S _____

_____

12. L S A M L T N I S I N E T E _____

10. Y D I K E N _____

_____

11. D L R E B A D _____

_____

13. S B O E N _____

14. N S I K _____

Name: _____ Date: _____

Body Systems

Webwise: www.innerbody.com (click on any body system)

Organs and tissues in the human body are organized into systems that work together to perform a specific function. Fill in the chart of some of the body systems by listing some principal parts of each system and what the primary function of the system is.

Body System	Principal Parts	Primary Function
Nervous System		
Circulatory System		
Respiratory System		
Digestive System		
Muscular System		
Skeletal System		
Excretory System		
Endocrine System		

Name: _____   Date: _____

Five Functions of Your Skeletal System

Far Out Fact: The human head contains 22 bones.

Webwise: Build a skeleton online at www.medtropolis.com/VBody.asp (click on skeleton)

No bones about it—your skeletal system is pretty important. Use the words in the word bank to fill in the blanks and see just what your bones do for you!

marrow	hard	muscles	protect
ribs	support	move	calcium
blood	shape	cells	skull
phosphorus			

1. The first function of your skeletal system is to give your body _____ and _____ it like the framework of a building.

2. The second function of your skeletal system is to help your body _____. Your major _____ are attached to your bones and facilitate movement.

3. The third function of your skeletal system is to _____ your major organs. Your brain in enclosed in the hard _____. Your heart and lungs are encased in your _____. Without this protection, any big bump or squish could kill you.

4. The fourth function of your skeletal system is to act like a factory. Inside some of your bones is a soft tissue called _____. This is where your body produces _____ _____.

5. As well as being a factory, your bones are also a warehouse. _____ and _____ compounds are stored there to use later. These substances are what make bones _____.

Name: _____ Date: _____

Bones by the Numbers

Far Out Fact: One quarter of the bones in your body are in your feet.

Solve these math riddles to learn about numbers and bones.

1. $(10 \times 12 \times 2) - 34 = a$ a = Number of bones in an adult human _____

2. $(17 + 18) \times (60 \div 6) = c$ c = Number of soft cartilage pieces a newborn has that later develop and fuse to make bones _____

3. $7(16 \div 4) = n$ n = Number of bones in a newborn's skull _____

4. $(9 \times 4) \div (30 \div 15) = m$ m = Number of months it takes for a baby's skull bones to close up _____

5. $(2 \times 2 \times 2 \times 2) - 2 = f$ f = Number of bones that shape your face _____

6. $(99 \div 9) + (136/136) = r$ r = Number of pairs of ribs in a human _____

7. $(2 \times 3 \times 9)/2 = h$ h = Number of bones in the human hand _____

8. $(2{,}697 \div 2{,}697)/4 = s$ s = Length (in inches) of the smallest bone in the body _____

9. $[4(5) + 8(5) + 2(2)] \div 8 = c$ c = Number of curved bones in your cranium _____

10. $[(3 \times 3) \times (8 + 3)] \div 3 = j$ j = Number of joints in each foot _____

Name: _____ Date: _____

Bizarre Bones

Far Out Fact: **Your thigh bone is stronger than concrete!**

Read over these interesting and unusual facts about bones and other parts of your skeletal system. Then find the **bold** words in the word search below.

1. Within the tendons that cover your knees are very small bones called **sesamoid** bones.

2. **Wormian** bones are found in the joints in your skull.

3. The **clavicle** is the most commonly broken bone in the body.

4. The **coccygeal** bones would be the beginning of a tail if you were an animal.

5. The **hyoid** bone (which supports your tongue) is the only bone not connected to another bone.

6. The "**funny bone**" is actually at the end of a bone called the **humerus**.

7. The smallest bone in your body is the **stirrup**, which is a tiny bone in your inner ear. It is only about 1/4" long.

8. Also in your inner ear, there is a bone called the **hammer** and one shaped like a snail's shell (the **cochlea**).

A	E	L	H	C	O	C	L	Y	N	L	U	P	L	L
F	O	R	H	Z	L	W	N	A	A	K	D	U	Y	X
O	V	L	S	H	J	A	I	E	W	L	N	R	G	L
F	U	S	N	C	G	M	G	H	I	B	P	R	P	Y
I	O	R	E	I	R	Y	N	A	U	N	O	I	P	U
M	B	F	X	O	C	E	K	Q	D	M	M	T	K	G
K	O	D	W	C	M	N	Q	J	I	Q	E	S	Q	P
H	O	F	O	T	X	O	S	L	O	G	E	R	V	R
B	A	C	N	Y	B	B	T	U	M	E	R	L	U	R
W	S	M	I	K	A	Y	K	V	A	I	D	T	B	S
A	Y	R	M	H	P	N	W	L	S	S	C	E	J	S
I	Z	L	Z	E	Y	N	A	X	E	H	P	X	E	C
M	N	V	W	D	R	U	V	I	S	G	L	T	G	S
X	K	O	G	C	N	F	C	L	A	V	I	C	L	E
J	R	H	Y	O	I	D	N	E	S	V	P	S	X	B

Bone Up on Bones

Are your bones alive? YES! They are living organs, composed of several types of tissue. They are much like any other organ.

- Bones have minerals—calcium and phosphorus provide strength and hardness.
- Bones have protein, which gives them their flexibility.
- Bones have nerves and blood vessels to feed the cells within them.
- Some bones have bone marrow. Red marrow is in flat bones and sometimes in the ends of long bones. Red marrow makes red and white blood cells and blood platelets. Yellow marrow, in the center of long bones, stores fat cells.

Check out the different parts of a bone...

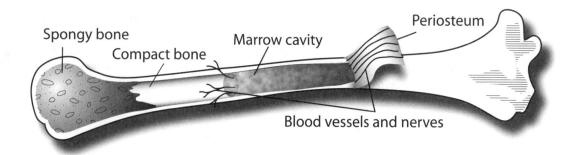

Periosteum: membrane that covers the surface of the bone; it has small blood vessels that bring nutrients into the bone

Compact bone: a hard layer of bone under the periosteum; contains blood vessels, bone cells, and deposits of protein, calcium, and phosphorus

Spongy bone: lightweight bone with small, open spaces (much like a sponge); found at the ends of longer bones

Marrow: found in the center of long bones and in the spaces of spongy bone; where blood cells are made

Cartilage: tissue on the end of bone that reduces friction; makes it easier for bones to move, and absorbs shocks

Ligaments: stretchy bands of tissue that hold bones together at joints (places where two or more bones meet)

Name: _____ Date: _____

What's in a Bone?

Complete the crossword puzzle using the clues below.

ACROSS

5. Lightweight bone filled with spaces

7. Tissue on bone ends that absorbs shocks and reduces friction

8. Gives bones some flexibility

9. Type of hard bone just under periosteum

DOWN

1. Membranes covering the surface of bones

2. Bands of tissue that hold bones together at joints

3. Places where bones meet

4. One of the minerals that makes bones hard

6. Tissue inside bones that makes blood cells

Name: _____ Date: _____

Shape Up Those Bones

Bones are classified into four groups: flat bones, long bones, short bones, and irregular bones. Each type of bone has a particular shape and function. Use the chart to help you tell which type each of these bones is.

Bone Type	Shape	Function
Flat Bones	Flat, often curved	Form protective wall around a body cavity
Long Bones	Long, tubular, enlarged ends	Provide support and protection, serve as levers
Short Bones	Like irregular cube shapes	Support weight, allow small movements
Irregular Bones	All other shapes	Variety of functions: protection, support, etc.

 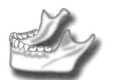

1. _____   2. _____   3. _____

4. _____   5. _____   6. _____

7. _____   8. _____   9. _____

Name: _____ Date: _____

What Bone Am I?

Far Out Fact: The word "skeleton" comes from an ancient Greek word that means "dried up."

Webwise: www.innerbody.com (click on the skeletal system)

   Use the reference illustration on page 16 to determine which bone is which. List both the scientific name and the common name.

1. The bony cage that protects your heart and lungs.

    _____   _____

2. The bone in the upper arm between the shoulder and the elbow.

    _____   _____

3. Large, thick bone that encases the brain to protect it.

    _____   _____

4. The bone in the upper leg between the hips and the knee.

    _____   _____

5. The bone that attaches to the skull like a hinge.

    _____   _____

6. The lower arm bone closest to the body.

    _____   _____

7. The lower arm bone farthest from the body.

    _____   _____

8. The larger of the two lower leg bones.

    _____   _____

9. The bone that runs across the top of the chest, between the shoulders.

    _____   _____

10. The bones of the foot just above the heel.

    _____   _____

11. The large, bowl-shaped bone connected to the top of the legs.

    _____   _____

12. The bones connecting the skull with the hipbone.

    _____   _____

Bare Bones

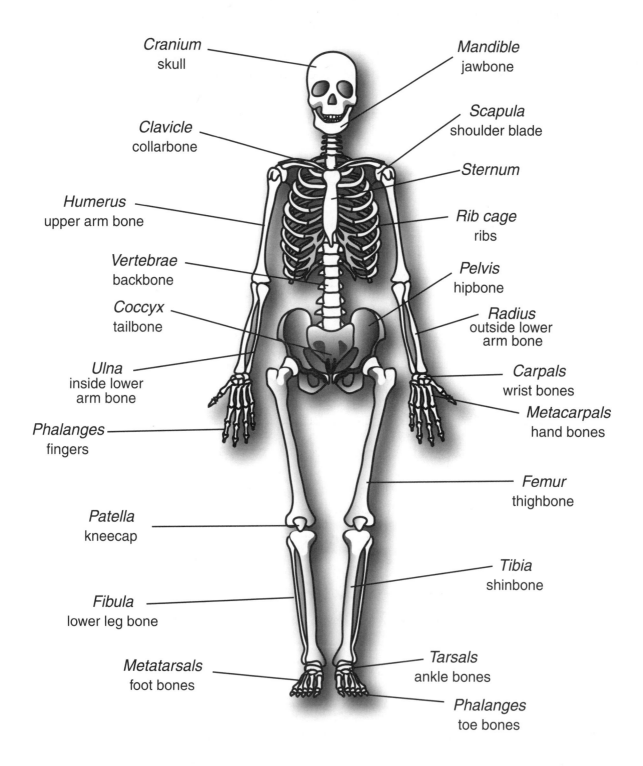

Cranium
skull

Mandible
jawbone

Clavicle
collarbone

Scapula
shoulder blade

Sternum

Humerus
upper arm bone

Rib cage
ribs

Vertebrae
backbone

Pelvis
hipbone

Coccyx
tailbone

Radius
outside lower
arm bone

Ulna
inside lower
arm bone

Carpals
wrist bones

Metacarpals
hand bones

Phalanges
fingers

Femur
thighbone

Patella
kneecap

Tibia
shinbone

Fibula
lower leg bone

Metatarsals
foot bones

Tarsals
ankle bones

Phalanges
toe bones

Double Duty

> **Far Out Fact:** Bone is six times stronger than a steel bar that weighs the same weight.

Your backbone has double duty to do.

Job 1: It provides the main upright support for your body.

When you are young, you have 33 **vertebrae** (the bone sections that stack up to make the spinal column). As you get older, some of the bones fuse together and become like one bone, so you end up with only 26 bones in your spine as an adult. Those that fuse are at the bottom of the spinal column.

The vertebrae are connected with **ligaments** (strong stretchy bands of tissue). In between each vertebrae is a disc of **cartilage** (soft, slippery tissue), which acts as a cushion.

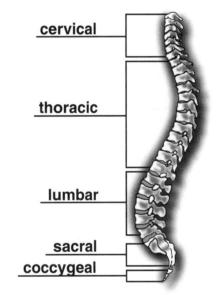

- The top seven are the **cervical vertebrae**. They hold your head and neck up.

- The next 12 are called the **thoracic vertebrae**. They are attached to your ribs.

- The next five are called the **lumbar vertebrae**. These are your lower back.

- At the bottom are 5 **sacral** and then 4 **coccygeal vertebrae**. These are the ones that fuse together.

Job 2: It protects your spinal cord.

Your spinal cord begins at the base of your brain and runs down a circular tube-like opening through the center of the spinal column. This tube is called the **spinal canal**.

Without the protection of the spinal column, the spinal cord would be severely injured with almost any bump, squish, or squeeze.

Name: _____ Date: _____

Odd Thing Out

Review your knowledge of the purpose and parts of the spinal column by finding the one word in each sentence that is incorrect and replacing it with the correct one.

1. The spinal canal is very delicate nerve tissue.

2. The sacral vertebrae are those that hold up the head and the neck.

3. The vertebrae are held together by strong cords called cartilage.

4. The coccygeal and thoracic vertebrae fuse together as you grow older.

5. The lumbar vertebrae are attached to your ribs.

6. Between each vertebrae is a disc of sacral that acts as a cushion.

7. The widest and largest vertebrae are the cervical vertebrae.

8. The tube where your spinal cord sits is called the lumbar canal.

9. The thoracic column protects the spinal cord from severe injury.

10. When you are young, your spinal column is made up of 26 vertebrae.

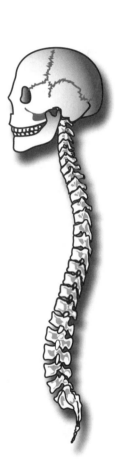

Joined Together

A place where two or more bones meet together is called a **joint**. At each joint, your bones have to be far enough apart not to rub against each other but still able to stay in place. A thick, smooth tissue called **cartilage** often covers the ends of bones at joints. It works like a slippery cushion, allowing bones to slide and reducing friction. Strong, stretchy bands of tissue called **ligaments** hold the bones of joints together. Some joints, like your knees, need several ligaments to do the job.

Joint Types

Immovable Joints *allow little or no movement*

Movable Joints *allow wide variety of movement*

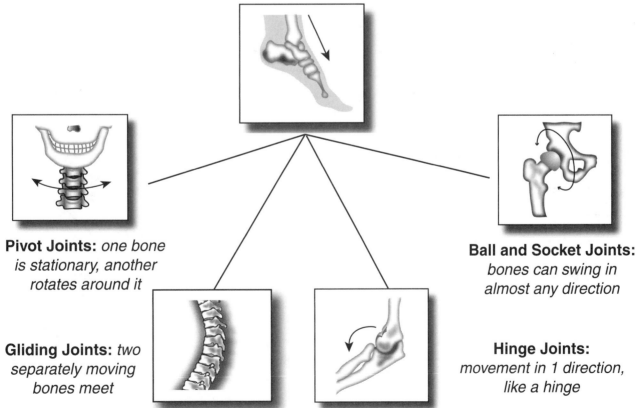

Pivot Joints: *one bone is stationary, another rotates around it*

Gliding Joints: *two separately moving bones meet*

Ball and Socket Joints: *bones can swing in almost any direction*

Hinge Joints: *movement in 1 direction, like a hinge*

Name: _____ Date: _____

Which Joint Do You Use?

For each activity, tell which type(s) of joint you use. If you use more than one, explain which part of the action uses which joint.

1. twisting your head around to look to the side

   _____

   _____

   _____

2. kicking a soccer ball

   _____

   _____

   _____

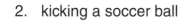

3. playing the piano

   _____

   _____

   _____

4. throwing a softball

   _____

   _____

   _____

5. bending over to pick up something

   _____

   _____

   _____

6. squatting to sit down

   _____

   _____

   _____

Name: _____ Date: _____

The Muscular System

Far Out Fact: The longest muscle in your body is the sartorius, which begins at your hip and stretches clear down to your knee.

Webwise: http://howstuffworks.com/muscle

A **muscle** is an organ that contracts and expands, creating movement. In your body, there are more than 600 muscles. Some of your muscles are very large and others are very small. Muscles not only help you move, but they also help give your body shape and produce heat in your body. Every minute of the day and night there are always some muscles moving in your body.

There are two main groups of muscles—the **voluntary muscles** and the **involuntary muscles**. Voluntary muscles are muscles that you control consciously (in other words, you think about when and how to move them). The involuntary muscles are those that work automatically (you don't have to think about them).

Look at each muscle listed below. Think about whether they move by themselves, without you having to think about it, or if they move because your brain tells them to. Put a "V" by those that are voluntary and an "I" by those that are involuntary.

_____ 1. heart   _____ 2. finger muscles

_____ 3. leg muscles   _____ 4. lungs

_____ 5. arm muscles   _____ 6. back muscles

_____ 7. stomach muscles   _____ 8. intestinal muscles

_____ 9. neck muscles   _____ 10. eye muscles that make you blink

11. Can you think of some muscles that sometimes work on their own, but which you can also choose to control for a time?

_____

_____

_____

_____

Name: _____ Date: _____

What Makes a Muscle?

Use the words in the box to fill in the blanks in this information about the makeup of muscles.

oxygen	cells	tendons	organ
fibers	bones	myosin	
signals	sliding	vessels	

Muscles are just like any other _____ because they are made up of groups of _____ and tissue working together. The basic muscle cell has two types of protein filaments called actin and _____. When a muscle is at work, these two filaments are _____ past each other.

Muscles have nerves through which they receive _____ from the brain to move. They also have blood _____ in them, through which they can receive the water, food, and _____ they need to stay alive.

Bundles of muscle cells (sometimes called muscle _____) are grouped together, surrounded by connective tissue.

Muscles are attached to the _____ with strong, stretchy bands of tissue called _____.

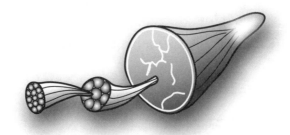

Types of Muscle Tissue

Far Out Fact: **Eye muscles move more than any other muscle ... maybe more than 100,000 times a day.**

Webwise: www.innerbody.com (click on the muscular system)

There are three types of muscle tissue in your body.

Skeletal muscles: These muscles move bones. They are attached to the bones with **tendons** (thick bands of tissue). They are the **voluntary** muscles (that you choose to move). They are the most common type of muscle in your body. Under a microscope, they look **striated** (or striped). They contract and relax quickly. Blood vessels bring them oxygen and food, and nerves connect to them to bring them the messages from your brain about when and how to move.

Smooth muscles: They are **involuntary** (work automatically). They are found in the walls of many of your organs, such as your intestines and blood vessels, and in your skin. They move the organs as needed. They contract and relax slowly. They are not striated. They are thin muscles. They have a nucleus in the middle of each cell.

Cardiac Muscles: This type of muscle is found only in the heart. It is **involuntary** (works on its own). Like skeletal muscle, it has striations, but the cells weave together a little differently. This type of muscle contracts nonstop all day and night for your whole life.

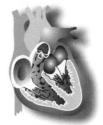
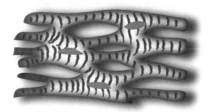

Name: _____ Date: _____

Muscle Up!

Far Out Fact: **The largest muscle in your body is the gluteus maximus (in your buttocks).**

Under each heading in the chart, list muscles in your body that are that type.

Skeletal Muscles	Smooth Muscles	Cardiac Muscles
1.	1.	1.
2.	2.	
3.	3.	
4.	4.	
5.	5.	

Why is it a good thing that not all of your muscles are voluntary?

_____

_____

_____

Move Those Muscles!

> **Far Out Fact:** The smallest muscle in your body is the stapedius, which is inside your ear.

So ... just how do all those skeletal muscles help our bodies move?

A skeletal muscle is hooked to a bone in two places. At one end, called the **origin**, the muscle is hooked directly to the bone. At the other end, called the **insertion**, the muscle is attached to the bone with a **tendon**—a very strong, stretchy band of tissue, sort of like a thick rubber band.

Muscles can't push, they only pull. Muscle movement always happens with pairs of muscles, pulling in opposite directions. Here's what happens when you bend your arm.

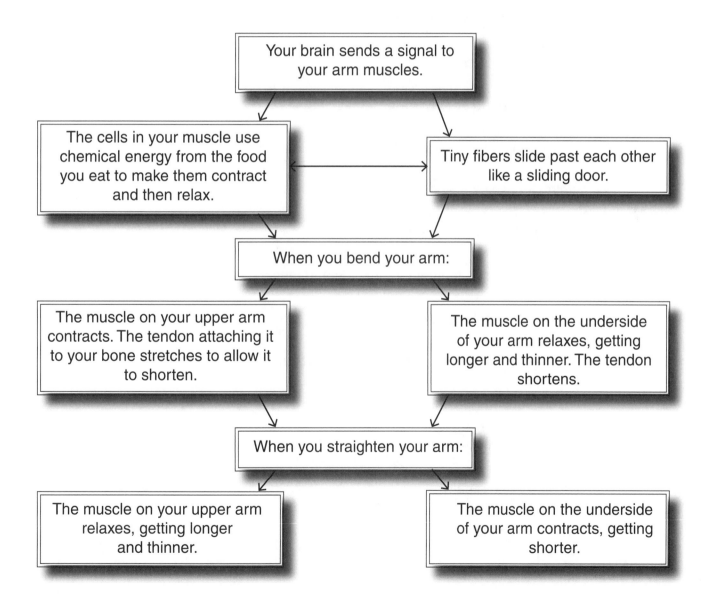

Name: _____ Date: _____

The Truth About Muscles

Far Out Fact: On average, 40% of your weight is from your muscles.

See if you remember what you have learned about muscles. Write "T" for true and "F" for false for each of these statements.

_____ 1. The human body has more than 600 muscles.

_____ 2. Muscles you tell when to move are called involuntary muscles.

_____ 3. The muscles in your foot are voluntary muscles.

_____ 4. Skeletal muscles are those that help you move.

_____ 5. Muscles are attached to bones with ligaments.

_____ 6. Smooth muscles are involuntary muscles.

_____ 7. The muscles in your stomach are smooth muscles.

_____ 8. Skeletal muscles are striated.

_____ 9. Your heart is a smooth muscle.

_____ 10. Cardiac muscle is found in your arms and legs.

_____ 11. Cardiac muscle is striated.

_____ 12. Tendons hook muscles to bone at the end called the insertion.

_____ 13. Muscles push and pull.

_____ 14. Muscles get their energy to move from the food you eat.

_____ 15. Muscles work in pairs.

_____ 16. When one muscle contracts, the opposite muscle relaxes.

Major Muscles

Far Out Fact: The strongest muscle in the human body, relative to its size, is the tongue.

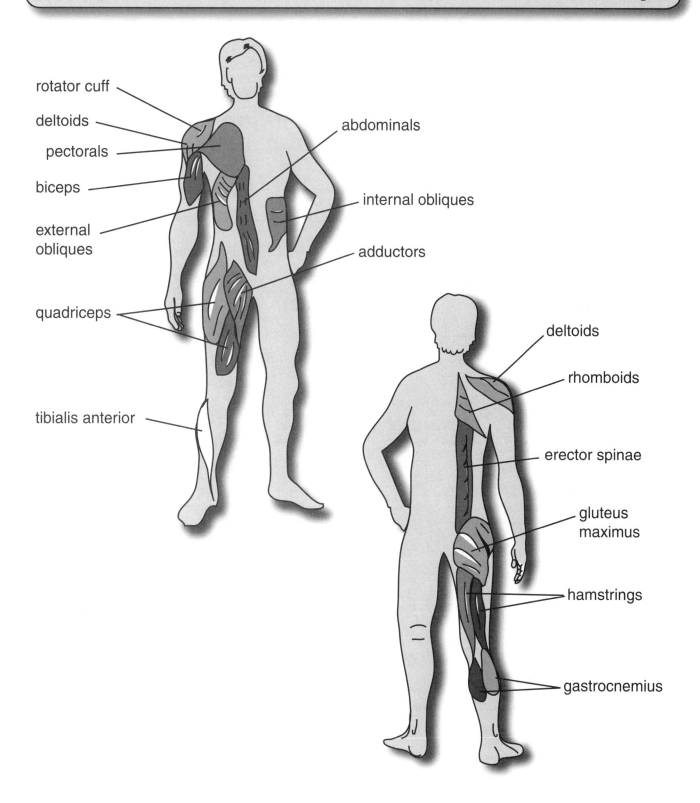

rotator cuff

deltoids

pectorals

biceps

external obliques

abdominals

internal obliques

adductors

quadriceps

tibialis anterior

deltoids

rhomboids

erector spinae

gluteus maximus

hamstrings

gastrocnemius

Name: _____ Date: _____

Mystery Muscles

Which muscle am I?

1. I am in the arm.

    I flex the elbow and move the forearm.

    I have 5 letters in my name.

    What muscle am I?

    _____

2. I am in the leg.

    I bend the knee.

    I am made of 3 muscles.

    What muscle(s) am I?

    _____

3. I am in the shoulder area.

    I raise and rotate the arm.

    There are 7 letters in my name.

    What muscle am I?

    _____

4. I am in the back.

    I extend the spine/trunk backwards.

    My name is two words.

    What muscle am I?

    _____

5. I am in the upper chest.

    I move the arm to the chest.

    I start with the letter "P"

    What muscle am I?

    _____

6. I am in the leg.

    I raise the front of the foot.

    I am also called the shin.

    What muscle am I?

    _____

7. I am in the thigh.

    I am made of 4 muscles.

    I extend the leg and knee.

    What muscle(s) am I?

    _____

8. I am low on the back of the body.

    I am one of the biggest muscles.

    I move the hips forward.

    What muscle am I?

    _____

Name: _____ Date: _____

Muscle Mastery

Write the underlined letters in the blanks below and then unscramble them to find the answers to these muscle questions.

1. The most im**p**ortant **m**uscle **i**nvolved in b**r**eathing is **a** sheet of thin, fl**a**t muscle that sits just below the lun**g**s. If this muscle gets irritate**d**, it might cause the **h**iccups. It is the

   — — — — — — — — —.   _____

2. If you forget to wa**r**m u**p** your muscles before you exer**c**ise, your **m**uscles might contr**a**ct involuntarily, which will cause a muscle

   — — — — —.   _____

3. A **c**hemical bui**l**d**u**p of this waste produ**c**t in the mus**c**le is what makes the muscles tired. **I**t occurs when the muscles **a**re working so hard **t**hat they don't rece**i**ve the **a**mount of oxygen they need. It is called

   — — — — — —   — — — —.   _____

4. If a **p**erson doesn'**t** use their muscles enough, they can become s**o**fter and weaker and actuall**y** **r**educe in size. **Th**is condition is c**a**lled

   — — — — — — —.   _____

5. If one of your **mu**scles start**s** to rapidly and re**p**eatedly contr**a**ct involuntarily, it is called a

   — — — — —.   _____

6. When a mu**s**cle, te**n**don, or ligament **is** **p**ulled and st**r**etched too much, it is called a

   — — — — — —.   _____

The Circulatory System

Far Out Fact: There are almost 60,000 miles of blood vessels in your body!

The circulatory system is also sometimes called the **cardiovascular system**. That name helps to describe the parts of this important system. **Cardio** means "heart" and **vascular** means "channels for conveying fluids"(vessels for blood in this case).Your cardiovascular system consists of your heart, your blood, and miles and miles of blood vessels that carry that blood to every cell in your body. The circulatory system has several jobs.

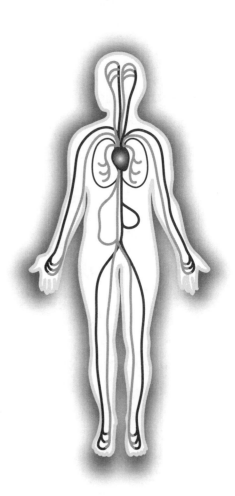

- **Job 1:** Every single cell in your body needs a continuous supply of oxygen and nutrients. There also must be a way for a cell's waste products to be removed from your body. Your heart pumps fresh, oxygenated blood through the body to supply your cells with oxygen and nutrients. The blook then picks up carbon dioxide and other wastes as it travels back to the heart.

- **Job 2:** The circulatory system helps your body maintain a controlled temperature. If you get very cold, the tiniest blood vessels, called capillaries, move down under the skin as far as they can go to stay close to your organs. If you get too hot, the capillaries move up as close to the surface of your skin as they can get, to give off some of the heat.

- **Job 3:** The circulatory system helps you fight off illnesses. Part of your blood consists of white blood cells, which are like an army of soldiers searching for and destroying germs and bacteria. They create antibodies, which protect against specific diseases.

- **Job 4:** The circulatory system delivers the chemicals from our food and medicines to the places they are needed.

Name: _____ Date: _____

Help Wanted!

Webwise: www.innerbody.com (click on the circulatory system)

Write a creative "help wanted" ad for the job of the circulatory system. Make sure you give a good description of the job requirements, hours, and expectations.

be experienced.
beautiful office
new building.
office skills and
arrangements
rly convention
Send resume &
ry requirements:
idburg Center
10702

ASSISTANT

school diploma,
assistance with
college tuition.
will train on the
Exciting career.
000-4009

NET JOBS

after-school job.
Fun atmosphere,
Responsible and
a plus. Call Mr.
appointment.

HELP WANTED
Circulatory System

_____

_____

_____

_____

_____

_____

_____

_____

_____

_____

_____

_____

_____

_____

_____

Work from
Your home
Or our off
Experience
A plus

HIRING 3

Wanted:
full time
Position
License

Health be
IRA invest
Vacation

Apply to:
P.O.Box 59

PART-TIME

NEW STORE NO
ACCEPTING APP
FOR PART-TIME
SALES PEOPLE
CALL MS. JOAN

Heart Parts

Far Out Fact: By the time you are 70, your heart will have beat around 2.5 billion times!

Webwise: Watch the process in action: http://www.pbs.org/wgbh/nova/body/map-human-heart.html

Or test yourself on heart parts: http://www.kidport.com/Grade6/Science/Heart.htm

Take a look at each part of the heart and what it does. Then use what you learn to help you do page 33.

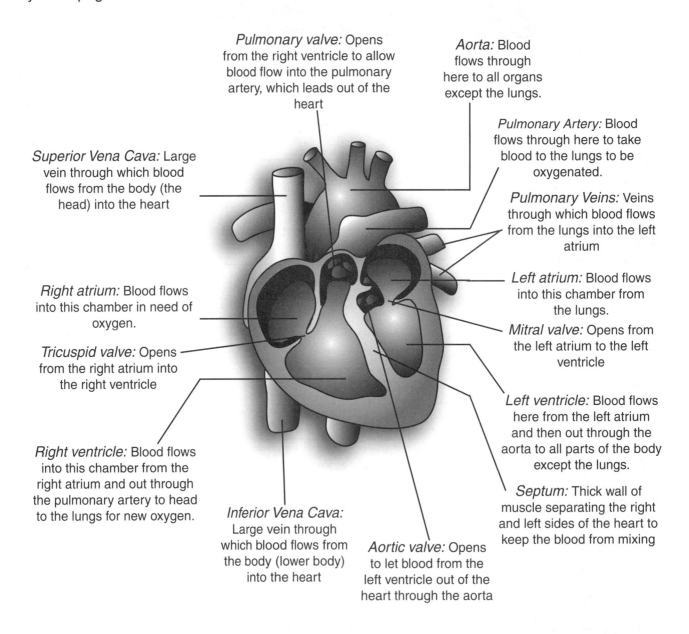

Pulmonary valve: Opens from the right ventricle to allow blood flow into the pulmonary artery, which leads out of the heart

Aorta: Blood flows through here to all organs except the lungs.

Pulmonary Artery: Blood flows through here to take blood to the lungs to be oxygenated.

Superior Vena Cava: Large vein through which blood flows from the body (the head) into the heart

Pulmonary Veins: Veins through which blood flows from the lungs into the left atrium

Left atrium: Blood flows into this chamber from the lungs.

Right atrium: Blood flows into this chamber in need of oxygen.

Mitral valve: Opens from the left atrium to the left ventricle

Tricuspid valve: Opens from the right atrium into the right ventricle

Left ventricle: Blood flows here from the left atrium and then out through the aorta to all parts of the body except the lungs.

Right ventricle: Blood flows into this chamber from the right atrium and out through the pulmonary artery to head to the lungs for new oxygen.

Septum: Thick wall of muscle separating the right and left sides of the heart to keep the blood from mixing

Inferior Vena Cava: Large vein through which blood flows from the body (lower body) into the heart

Aortic valve: Opens to let blood from the left ventricle out of the heart through the aorta

Name: _____ Date: _____

Blood Flow

Far Out Fact: **Your heart is about as big as a fist when you are a child and about as big as two fists when you are an adult.**

Webwise: Watch a slide show of the flow of blood through the heart at
http://www.childrensheartinstitute.org/blood-flow-slideshow

Use page 32 to help you describe the flow of blood through the heart. Note: Some words may be used more than once.

septum	tricuspid	mitral
pulmonary	aortic	atrium
ventricle	vena cava	aorta

First, blood that is returning from the body is in need of oxygen. It travels through the superior and inferior _____ and into the right _____, which contracts when it is full. This opens the _____ valve, allowing the blood to rush into the right _____.

When this chamber contracts, it pushes open the _____ valve, and blood is squeezed into the _____ arteries. From there, it travels to the lungs. In the lungs, the carbon dioxide wastes are released, and the blood receives oxygen. Once it has received new oxygen, the blood travels through the _____ veins and into the left _____.

From there, the _____ valve opens, and the blood rushes into the left _____. The contraction of this chamber of the heart pushes open the _____ valve, and the oxygen-filled blood travels into the largest artery of the body called the _____.

From there, it will be delivered to every cell in your body. The whole time, the oxygen-poor blood and oxygen-rich blood are kept separated by a thick muscle wall called the _____.

Everything in Threes

> *Far Out Fact:* **Even when you are resting, your heart muscles work twice as hard as your leg muscles do when you are sprinting.**

Webwise: www.medtropolis.com/VBody.asp (click on heart)

Three Types of Circulation

Scientists have divided your circulation into three sections.

Pulmonary Circulation: The circulation of blood as it travels through the heart, to the lungs, where it picks up oxygen and travels back to the heart, after which it is pushed into the aorta

Systemic Circulation: The circulation of newly oxygenated blood as it travels to all the body tissues and organs, delivering oxygen and nutrients, picking up carbon dioxide and other waste products, and making its way back to the heart

Coronary Circulation: The circulation of blood through the coronary arteries to the tissues of the heart itself, supplying it with the required nutrients and oxygen

Three Types of Blood Vessels

Arteries: Blood vessels that carry blood away from the heart—They attach to the ventricles in the heart. Some major arteries are the pulmonary arteries, which carry blood from the heart to the lungs, and the aorta, which carries blood from the heart to the rest of the body. The aorta divides and branches out into smaller arteries to reach each region of the body. Arteries have thick, tough outer walls and smooth inner walls.

Veins: Blood vessels that carry blood toward the heart—Blood in veins carries waste products, such as carbon dioxide, and is low in oxygen. Veins have valves in them that keep blood flowing toward the heart. The walls of veins are thinner than those of arteries.

Capillaries: Microscopic blood vessels that connect arteries to veins—Nutrients and oxygen diffuse through capillary walls to the cells, and waste products move from the cells into the capillaries. The walls of capillaries are only one cell thick.

Name: _____ Date: _____

Circulation True and False

Use what you learned on page 34 to tell if each of these statements is true or false. Write "T" for true and "F" for false.

_____ 1. Blood traveling to all the areas of the body to deliver nutrients and oxygen is called coronary circulation.

_____ 2. The heart itself requires nutrients and oxygen, which are supplied through coronary arteries.

_____ 3. Arteries carry blood away from the heart.

_____ 4. The walls of capillaries are one cell thick.

_____ 5. Pulmonary circulation is the path of blood as it travels from the heart to the lungs to become oxygenated.

_____ 6. Blood in veins is rich in oxygen.

_____ 7. Blood is transferred from arteries to veins through capillaries.

_____ 8. The aorta is an artery.

_____ 9. Veins have valves to help them keep blood pushing toward the heart.

_____ 10. Arteries have thick, rough inner walls.

_____ 11. Systemic circulation supplies nutrients and oxygen to the heart.

_____ 12. The larger arteries divide and branch off into smaller arteries.

_____ 13. The blood in veins carries waste products back to the heart and lungs.

_____ 14. The walls in veins are thicker than those in arteries.

_____ 15. Capillaries are the tiniest of the blood vessels.

Name: _____ Date: _____

Blood, Blood, and More Blood

Far Out Fact: Half of the red blood cells in your body are replaced every week.

Blood consists of cells, cell fragments, and liquid. It is made up of four parts:

Red Blood Cells: Disc-shaped cells containing a protein called hemoglobin—They deliver oxygen and remove carbon dioxide. Two to three million red blood cells are made in the marrow of long bones every second. They live for about 120 days and then die out. They have no nuclei. One cubic millimeter of blood contains 5 million red blood cells.

White Blood Cells: Come in various shapes and sizes—They are made in the spleen and the lymph nodes. They destroy bacteria, viruses, and foreign substances. When you have an infection, your body creates extra white blood cells. One cubic millimeter of blood contains around 5 to 10 thousand white blood cells. White blood cells live from several days to several months.

Platelets: Irregular shaped fragments of protoplasm—They are not living cells. They circulate with the red and white blood cells. They help the blood clot. Platelets last in the blood for 5–9 days. A cubic millimeter of blood has up to 400 thousand platelets.

Plasma: The liquid part of blood—It is mostly water. Oxygen, nutrients, and minerals are also dissolved in plasma. Blood is more than half plasma. Plasma carries dissolved foods to your cells.

For each item below, write "R" if it is true of red blood cells, "W" if it is true of white blood cells, "PT" if it is true of platelets, or "PM" if it is true of plasma.

_____ 1. kills viruses

_____ 2. carries oxygen

_____ 3. is mostly water

_____ 4. lasts 5–9 days in the blood

_____ 5. made in spleen

_____ 6. contains hemoglobin

_____ 7. is disc shaped

_____ 8. helps blood clot

_____ 9. half of blood is this

_____ 10. made in bone marrow

_____ 11. are cell fragments

_____ 12. 5 million in mm^3 of blood

_____ 13. minerals dissolved in it

_____ 14. not living cells

_____ 15. comes in varied shapes

_____ 16. up to 10,000 in mm^3 of blood

_____ 17. has no nuclei

_____ 18. lives 120 days on average

The Lymphatic System

Webwise: www.innerbody.com (click on lymphatic system)

The **lymphatic system** is another system that carries fluids in your body and uses vessels and capillaries. Let's look at what the lymphatic system does.

- In between your cells is a tissue fluid that contains dissolved substances and some of the water that comes out of your blood. This extra fluid is collected by the lymphatic system and then returned to the blood through lymph capillaries and vessels that carry it to large veins near the heart.

- The lymphatic system also helps fight off disease-causing organisms. It produces **lymphocytes** (a type of white blood cell) that fight infections and attack other foreign substances.

- Once the extra body fluids enter the lymphatic capillaries, it is known as lymph. **Lymph** is moved around the body with skeletal muscle contractions and contractions of smooth muscles in the lymph vessels. Lymph vessels have valves to prevent the backward flow of lymph, just as veins do in the circulatory system.

- **Lymph nodes** are bean-shaped structures through which the lymph passes before it returns to the blood. Here is where microorganisms and foreign materials are filtered. Major lymph nodes include the **tonsils** (at the back of your mouth), the **thymus** (behind your scapula) and the **spleen** (behind the upper left part of the stomach).

- The spleen is the largest lymph node. It filters blood and breaks down damaged red blood cells. Bacteria and other foreign substances are also destroyed by special cells in the spleen.

- The thymus produces lymphocytes, which are then sent to other organs in the lymphatic system.

- When you have an infection, your lymph nodes often swell up. The doctor might feel them in your neck or in your armpits. This happens because the lymphocytes, which engulf and destroy bacteria, fill the nodes.

Name: _____ Date: _____

Faulty Lymphatic Facts

Each sentence has one word that is inaccurate. Find it, cross it out, and replace it with a correct word.

1. The lymphatic system collects extra blood that is between the cells.

2. The lymphatic system produces capillaries, which help fight off infection.

3. Once the fluid enters the lymphatic capillaries, it is known as nodes.

4. Lymphocytes are a type of red blood cell.

5. Lymph is moved through the body by stretching of the skeletal muscles.

6. The largest lymph node in the body is the thymus.

7. Microorganisms and foreign materials are filtered in the lymph vessels.

8. The thymus lies behind the scapula and destroys lymphocytes.

9. The spleen breaks down new red blood cells and destroys bacteria.

10. If your lymph nodes are swollen, you likely have an aneurysm.

Name: _____ Date: _____

Yum!

Far Out Fact: You cannot taste food unless it is mixed with saliva.

Nutrients are substances found in foods that your body needs to function. Scientists have classified nutrients into six categories. Fill in the missing vowels to find out what they are and then read how each one is important to your health and well being.

C __ r b __ h y d r __ t __ s:
provide energy for all body functions

P r __ t __ __ n s:
used for growth and repair of body tissues

V __ t __ m __ n s:
help regulate body functions, build cells

M __ n __ r __ l s:
build cells, take part in chemical reactions, carry oxygen, and send nerve impulses

F __ t s:
store energy, help absorb some vitamins and cushion organs

W __ t __ r:
carries other substances, enables chemical reactions, removes waste products from cells

1. What might happen if you only ate one kind of food?

   _____

   _____

   _____

2. On a separate paper make a menu of a well-balanced meal. For each food in your meal, list the category (or categories) of nutrients it is made from and what function it will serve for your body.

Name: _____ Date: _____

The Digestive System

Far Out Fact: Honey is very easy for humans to digest because it has already been digested by a bee.

Webwise: www.innerbody.com (click on the digestive system)

Humans are consumers. We need to eat food to get fuel to help our bodies run. There are three reasons we need this fuel.

#1: For energy: Everything we do requires energy—walking, talking, blinking, breathing, thinking, etc.

#2: To build our bodies: Building bones, muscles, skin, hair, and all the other tissues in our bodies requires food to provide the building materials.

#3: To repair damaged tissues: Growing new skin over wounds, replacing old blood cells or lost blood, and fixing broken bones or blood vessels—the materials to do this come from the food we eat also.

Digestion is the process our bodies use to break down the food we eat so that it can be used for energy or building and repairing materials. The digestive system includes all of the organs that contribute to this process.

Circle all of the things below that are part of the digestive system.

stomach	tongue	mouth	salivary glands
heart	bladder	liver	rectum
eyes	gall bladder	lungs	pancreas
teeth	esophagus	saliva	skull
spleen	large intestine	kidneys	spinal cord

Name: _____ Date: _____

Coming Through

Number these steps in order to explain how the process of digestion occurs.

A. _____ The soft mass of food enters the stomach.

B. _____ The chyme enters the **duodenum** (the first part of the small intestine).

C. _____ You chew—your tongue and teeth break the food into smaller pieces.

D. _____ Digestive juices from the liver and pancreas are added, which breaks down the food more.

E. _____ The remaining materials that were not absorbed pass into the large intestine.

F. _____ You put some food into your mouth.

G. _____ **Peristalsis** (muscular contractions that move the food) mixes the chyme in the intestine.

H. _____ Cells on the surface of the **villi** (tiny projections on the walls of the small intestine) absorb the molecules of nutrients from the soupy chyme.

I. _____ Contractions of the esophagus (called **peristalsis**) squeeze the food downward.

J. _____ Excess water is absorbed from the mass of undigested material.

K. _____ The blood transports the nutrients to all the cells in the body.

L. _____ The food is mixed with saliva, which has an enzyme called **salivary amylase** that begins the breakdown of starch to sugar.

M. _____ In the stomach, food is mixed by the movement of the stomach walls.

N. _____ Strong digestive juices (produced by cells in the stomach walls) also mix with the food in the stomach, until it is a watery substance called **chyme**.

O. _____ The waste is then excreted from your body by muscles in the rectum and anus.

P. _____ The stomach expands and its folds smooth out.

Q. _____ Your tongue moves the food to the back of your mouth where it is swallowed, passing into the esophagus.

R. _____ The molecules of nutrients pass into blood vessels in the villi.

Name: _____ Date: _____

Mechanical vs. Chemical Digestion

Far Out Fact: **Your stomach has to make a new layer of mucus every two weeks or it would digest itself.**

Webwise: www.medtropolis.com/VBody.asp (click on digestive system)

There are two types of digestion that are going on as your food passes through your digestive system. Both change the food that you eat.

Mechanical digestion: when food is changed physically by chewing, chopping into smaller bits, separating parts, moving from one place to another, or mixing parts together

Chemical digestion: when food is changed chemically; when acids, bases, and enzymes work on the carbohydrates, proteins, and fats in your food and change it into smaller molecules to deliver nutrients to your cells

Both types of digestion occur in several places in the digestive system. Look at the list of steps in the digestive process from page 41. List several places where each type of digestion occurs.

Mechanical digestion   **Chemical digestion**

_____   _____

_____   _____

_____   _____

_____   _____

_____   _____

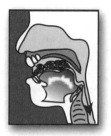

Know Your Digestive Organs

Far Out Fact: You produce around 10,000 gallons of saliva in a lifetime.

Learn more about each of the specific organs involved in the process of digestion by studying the information on this page and page 44. Then use the information to complete the activities on pages 45 and 46.

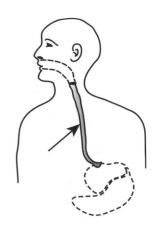

Esophagus: This organ is a tube in your throat that squeezes the food down into the stomach by using pulses of contracting muscle (called **peristalsis**). It is next to the **trachea** (through which air travels to your lungs). When not in use, the esophagus is flat, but it stretches open when you swallow food. When you swallow, a flap of tissue called the **epiglottis** automatically covers the top of the trachea so that food will not go into your lungs but will enter the esophagus. Should you happen to swallow air through your esophagus, it will come back out as a burp.

Stomach: This bag-like organ is where the food is further digested to change it to a form that can be absorbed into the bloodstream. In the stomach, the chewed-up food is churned and mixed with gastric juices (enzymes, hydrochloric acid (HCl), and mucus). Food remains in the stomach for two to six hours, until it is sufficiently broken down. The resulting mixture is called **chyme**. Like the esophagus, the stomach also expands when it is full and contracts when it is empty. The walls of the stomach are lined with a thick layer of mucus that protects it from its own acids so that it does not digest itself. This mucus periodically replaces itself.

Small Intestine: The small intestine is the longest part of the digestive system. It is only called the small intestine because it is thinner than the large intestine or colon. When the chyme leaves the stomach, it passes into the **duodenum** (the first section of the small intestine). Digestive juices from the pancreas, liver, and gallbladder are added to those in the intestine and begin to break apart the fats, carbohydrates, and proteins. Then the chyme passes through the **jejunum** and the **ilium** (the other sections of the small intestine) where the work of digestion is completed. Nutrients are completely broken down and are small enough to be absorbed by the millions of tiny **villi** (finger-like projections that line the walls of the folds in the small intestine). Nutrients move into the capillaries surrounding the villi and are carried into the bloodstream to all the cells in the body.

Know Your Digestive Organs (cont.)

Far Out Fact: When you are resting, your liver filters 6 cups of blood every minute.

Large Intestine: Once the nutrients are absorbed and carried into the bloodstream, the remaining materials move into the large intestine (or colon). Here, remaining water is absorbed from the waste and carried to the cells of the body. What is left (called **feces**) is stored in the rectum until it is full and then expelled from the body through the **anus**.

Salivary glands: There is a set of six salivary glands. The **submaxillary glands** are located under the lower jaw, the **sublingual glands** are found under the tongue, and the **parotids** are in front of the ears. These glands produce **saliva**, which is a liquid that begins to digest starches by breaking them down into sugars and also softens the food before swallowing.

Liver: The liver performs a large number of important functions in the process of digestion. It produces a substance called **bile** that breaks down fats into smaller molecules. It processes nutrients and separates them. It filters wastes or toxins from the blood and helps control the blood sugar level in your body.

Liver

Pancreas: This organ produces **enzymes** that travel through the **pancreatic duct** into the small intestine, where they break down carbohydrates, fats, and proteins. It also secretes an alkaline solution that helps to neutralize the acid in the stomach. The pancreas is not only part of the digestive system, but also a part of the endocrine system, where it produces hormones, such as insulin, that keep the blood sugar level in the body balanced.

Gallbladder: This small organ stores the bile the liver produces and sends it into the small intestine as needed. There, the bile, which is a fluid containing special salts, breaks up fat particles from foods. However, you can survive without your gallbladder.

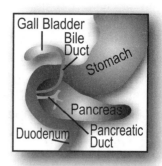

Gall Bladder
Bile
Duct
Stomach
Pancreas
Duodenum   Pancreatic
Duct

Name: _____ Date: _____

Whose Job Is It?

Use the information from pages 43 and 44 to help you decide which organ or tissue performs each job listed below in the clues.

esophagus	salivary glands	saliva	stomach	liver
pancreas	gall bladder	anus	epiglottis	rectum
duodenum	small intestine	bile	villi	chyme
peristalsis	large intestine			

_____ 1. We secrete a liquid to help soften food as you chew it.

_____ 2. I squeeze food down into the stomach.

_____ 3. I store bile made by the liver until it is needed.

_____ 4. I am where chyme is mixed with bile and other enzymes produced by the liver and pancreas.

_____ 5. I cover the trachea so food doesn't enter the lungs.

_____ 6. I am the liquid that first begins to digest starches.

_____ 7. I am the wavelike muscle contractions that move food down the esophagus and through the digestive system.

_____ 8. I am where food is churned and mixed with gastric juices that begin to digest it.

_____ 9. I produce enzymes that break down fats, carbohydrates, and proteins and hormones that regulate the body.

_____ 10. We line the walls of the small intestine and absorb the nutrients that have been digested.

_____ 11. I am where leftover wastes are stored before expulsion from the body.

_____ 12. I am a fluid that contains special salts that break up fat particles.

_____ 13. I am where wastes are expelled from the body.

_____ 14. I filter blood, produce bile, process and separate nutrients, and help regulate the body's blood sugar.

_____ 15. I am where excess water is removed from the material left over after the digested nutrients are absorbed.

_____ 16. I am the thin, watery material left when digestion in the stomach is complete.

_____ 17. I am the longest tube, through which chyme passes as it is further digested and the nutrients are absorbed to be taken to the body cells.

Name: _____ Date: _____

What's Where?

Use the information from pages 43 and 44 to help you label the parts of the digestive system with words from the word bank and tell the primary function of each part.

stomach	esophagus	rectum
salivary glands	large intestine	liver
small intestines	gall bladder	pancreas

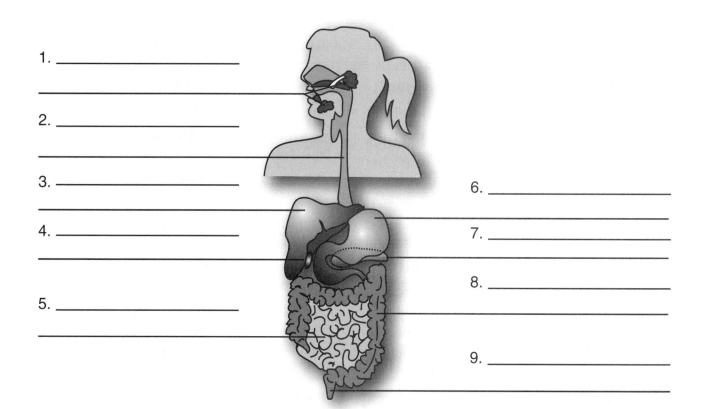

1. _____

_____

2. _____

_____

3. _____

_____

4. _____

_____

5. _____

_____

6. _____

7. _____

8. _____

9. _____

The Respiratory System

Far Out Fact: The surface area inside your lungs is large enough to cover a tennis court.

Webwise: http://science.nationalgeographic.com/science/health-and-human-body/human-body/lungs-article.html

Your respiratory system has two main jobs.

#1: Take in oxygen from the air to pass to the blood so that it can reach each cell in the body

#2: Remove waste gases that come from the body's cells

Quick Overview of Breathing Process

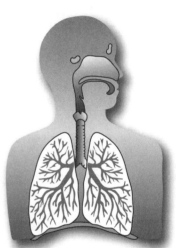

Step 1: Your diaphragm contracts and moves down as you breathe in.

Step 1a: As you inhale, air enters your body through the nose and mouth.

Step 2: Air then travels down through the trachea and into the lungs.

Step 3: Two bronchi branch off the trachea and carry the oxygen further into the lungs.

Step 4: Thousands of tiny tubes called bronchioles branch off from the bronchi and carry the oxygen even deeper into the lungs.

Step 5: The oxygen then inflates the millions of tiny air sacs called alveoli, which are clustered at the ends of the bronchioles.

Step 6: Oxygen passes from the air into the capillaries that surround the alveoli, where it can return to the heart and be pumped throughout the body.

Step 7: The waste gas carbon dioxide passes from the blood into the alveoli, where it is expelled from the body as you exhale.

Step 7a: Your diaphragm expands and moves up as you breathe out.

Name: _____ Date: _____

Travelogue

Imagine that you are a molecule of oxygen that is inhaled and makes its way through the respiratory system and circulatory system and to a body cell. Write a brief travelogue on this postcard describing your trip to a friend.

Now imagine you are a molecule of carbon dioxide that is leaving a body cell and traveling back through the circulatory system and respiratory system and is exhaled. Write a description of your travels on this postcard.

Respiratory Parts and Pieces

Far Out Fact: You breathe in and out about 22,000 times per day.

Webwise: www.innerbody.com (click on respiratory system)

Learn more about each of the specific organs and tissues involved in the respiratory process by studying the information on this page and page 50. Then use the information to complete the puzzle on page 51.

Nasal cavity: Air enters your nose through two holes called **nostrils**, as well as through your mouth, and enters your nasal cavity. Tiny hairs called **cilia** trap dust from the air, and **mucus** that lines your nasal cavity traps even more dirt, pollen, and other materials you don't want in your lungs. As the air passes through your nasal cavity, it is warmed from the tiny blood vessels in your nose and moistened. The materials filtered out by the mucus and hairs are moved by the cilia to the back of the throat where they can be swallowed or sometimes coughed or sneezed out.

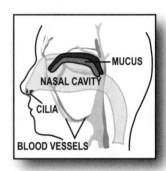

Pharynx (also called the throat): This is a tube that connects to the trachea. Cilia in the pharynx continue the job of filtering dirt, dust, or bacteria that wasn't caught before.

Epiglottis: This is a flap of tissue at the end of the pharynx that covers the top of the glottis (the opening between your vocal cords) when you swallow—making sure your food goes down your esophagus and into your stomach and not down your trachea and into your lungs.

Larynx (also called the voice box): Your vocal cords are attached to this airway. When you speak, whisper, yell, or sing, your muscles tighten and loosen the vocal cords. When air from your lungs passes over them, they vibrate and different pitches of sound are produced.

Trachea (also called the windpipe): Air travels down this tube on its way to the lungs. It is also lined with mucus and cilia to continue to trap dirt, dust, and other materials. C-shaped rings of cartilage keep the trachea open at all times. They are the bumps you feel if you tilt your head back and rub your hand up and down your neck.

Respiratory Parts and Pieces (cont.)

Far Out Fact: Your left lung is smaller than your right lung to leave room for your heart.

Lungs: These are two cone-shaped organs filled with layers of what look like spongy material. It is actually an intricate latticework of tubes. The right lung has three lobes, and the left has only two (to leave room for the heart). The lungs consist of the bronchi, the bronchioles, and the alveoli.

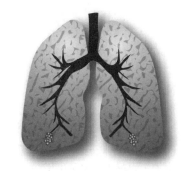

Bronchi: The base of the trachea splits into two tubes called **bronchi** (each one alone is a bronchus). These tubes carry the air you breathe further into the lungs.

Bronchioles: Each bronchi branches off further into thousands of smaller and smaller tubes that carry the air even further into the lungs.

Alveoli: These are clusters of tiny air sacs at the end of the smallest bronchioles. They are extremely thin (only one cell thick) and are surrounded by capillaries. Oxygen from the air **diffuses** (passes) from the alveoli into the capillaries where it can travel back to the heart and the body cells. Carbon dioxide waste from the blood cells diffuses from the capillaries into the alveoli, where it can be expelled from the lungs when you exhale.

Diaphragm: This is a muscle that sits just below the lungs, separating them from the abdomen. This muscle contracts and relaxes as you breathe. As you inhale, the diaphragm contracts and moves down, increasing the volume of your chest cavity so there is room for your lungs to fill with air. As you exhale, the diaphragm relaxes and moves up, pushing air out of your lungs and returning them to their original position.

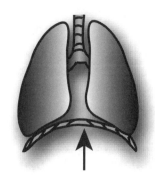

Name: _____ Date: _____

Take a Deep Breath!

Complete the crossword puzzle using the clues below.

ACROSS

1. flap that covers larynx and trachea when you swallow

5. tiny branches of tubes that carry air deep into the lungs

9. your voice box—where your vocal cords are

10. tiny hairs that trap dust and pollens

DOWN

2. your throat—at the base of the nasal cavity

3. muscle below lungs that expands and contracts as you breathe

4. tiny air sacs at the end of bronchioles, where exchange of oxygen and carbon dioxide takes place

6. tiny blood vessels that surround alveoli

7. two tubes that branch off from the trachea

8. your windpipe; carries air to the lungs

Name: _____ Date: _____

Breathing vs. Respiration

Aren't breathing and respiration the same thing? No!

Breathing is the process where fresh air is brought into the lungs, bringing oxygen to the circulatory system and the cells, and stale air is removed from the lungs, expelling the carbon dioxide wastes produced by the cells.

Respiration is a process that takes place within the cells. The digestive system produces glucose in the cells from digested food. Oxygen combines with glucose in a chemical reaction that releases energy. This process is called respiration. A waste product of respiration is carbon dioxide, which is carried back to your lungs and expelled when you exhale.

Circle the fact that is true in each pair.

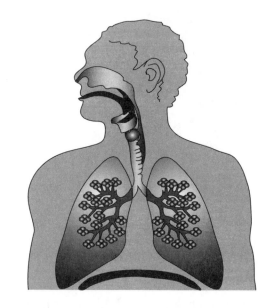

1. a. Fresh air entering your lungs and stale air leaving is part of breathing.

    b. Fresh air entering your lungs and stale air leaving is part of respiration.

2. a. Respiration happens in the lungs.

    b. Respiration happens in the cells.

3. a. Expelling carbon dioxide produces energy during respiration.

    b. A chemical reaction between oxygen and glucose produces energy during respiration.

4. a. Respiration involves three systems: respiratory, circulatory, and digestive.

    b. Respiration involves only the respiratory system.

Name: _____ Date: _____

The Excretory System

Far Out Fact: Your kidneys filter your blood as many as 400 times per day!

Webwise: http://www.kidshealth.org/kid/htbw/kidneys.html

The job of the excretory system is to rid the body of wastes.

Solid wastes are removed from the body as part of the digestive system. When the nutrients have been removed from the food you eat, the remaining material moves into the large intestine. There, excess water is removed and what is left is stored in the rectum until it is full. Then it is expelled through the anus.

Gaseous wastes are removed from the body as part of the respiratory system. Waste gases from the blood travel to the lungs and diffuse into the alveoli in the lungs. They are then expelled when you exhale.

Liquid wastes are removed from the body as part of the urinary system and by the skin. These are what you will learn about in this section.

Put each of these words under the correct heading to indicate if they are related to the urinary tract or related to the skin.

ureter	dermis	epidermis	bladder
sweat glands	kidneys	urethra	pores

Urinary Tract   **Skin**

_____   _____

_____   _____

_____   _____

_____   _____

The Urinary Tract

Far Out Fact: Your urine is yellow because of the bile in it.

Webwise: www.innerbody.com (click on the urinary system)

The urinary tract consists of four principal parts. Study the material on this page and on page 55 to learn about the urinary system. Then use the information to complete the activity on page 56.

Kidneys: There is one on each side of your body. All of your blood passes through your kidneys hundreds of times a day, and the wastes are removed by tiny filters called nephrons. Purified blood is returned to your circulatory system, and the waste liquid (urine) that is left behind flows into collecting tubules in each kidney.

Ureters: The urine collected in the kidneys drips into the ureters, which are tubes connecting to the bladder.

Urethra: When you urinate, the urine travels from your bladder through this tube and out of your body.

Bladder: This is an elastic storage sac that holds the urine from the kidneys. It can stretch to hold about a pint of urine, but when it is about half full, it will send a signal to your brain that you need to go.

A Closer Look at Your Kidneys

Normally you have two kidneys, one on each side of your body.

- If you put your hands on your hips and slide them up until you feel your ribs, your kidneys are about where your thumbs lie.

- They are shaped like kidney beans and are approximately 5 inches (13 cm) long and 3 inches (8 cm) thick.

- They are surrounded by fat for protection and to keep them in place.

- Blood enters the kidneys by way of a large renal artery and exits through a large renal vein.

- Inside each kidney are around a million **nephrons** (tiny filtering units).

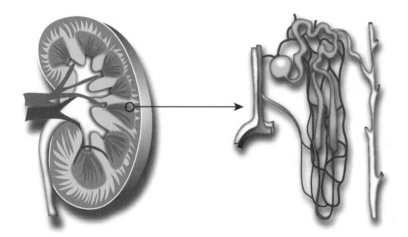

A Closer Look at a Nephron

- Nephrons consist of a bowl-shaped structure and a tubule that serves as a collecting duct.

- Inside the bowl-shaped structure are capillaries (tiny blood vessels). They carry blood that needs filtering from the arteries.

- Water, salts, sugar, and wastes from your blood pass into the bowl-shaped structure.

- Liquid is squeezed into the tubules, where capillaries surrounding them reabsorb needed water, salts, and sugar and send them back in the purified blood. Unneeded materials and waste flow into the collecting tubules to make their way to the bladder and out of your body.

Name: _____ Date: _____

Urinary System True or False

Far Out Fact: You can survive with only one kidney.

Write "T" for true or "F" for false.

_____ 1. Your liver is part of the urinary system.

_____ 2. All of the blood in your body passes through your kidneys once a day.

_____ 3. The main job of the kidneys is to filter your blood.

_____ 4. Waste liquid is called urine.

_____ 5. Urine travels from your kidneys to your bladder in the urethra.

_____ 6. Your bladder stretches to hold the urine until you pee.

_____ 7. Urine travels out of your body through the urethra.

_____ 8. Fat around the kidneys helps protect them.

_____ 9. Filtered blood leaves your kidneys through a renal artery.

_____ 10. There are 100 nephrons in each kidney.

_____ 11. Capillaries carry blood into the nephrons.

_____ 12. Water, salts, and sugars pass into bowl-shaped structures in the nephrons.

_____ 13. Unneeded materials and waste travel to a collecting tubule, which is part of the nephron.

_____ 14. Capillaries reabsorb needed water, salts, and sugars from the nephron.

_____ 15. Blood leaves the kidneys through a renal vein and returns to the main circulatory system.

Name: _____ Date: _____

The Skin

> **Far Out Fact:** Your skin is the largest organ of your body.

Your skin also plays a role in the excretory system. The top layer of your skin contains millions of sweat glands. When you sweat, excess water, salt, and **urea** (a protein) are released.

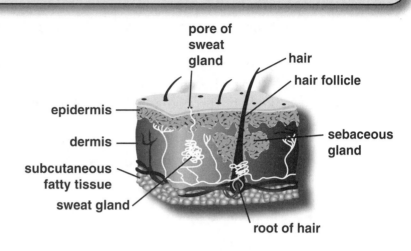

Use the words in the box to fill in the blanks in this paragraph about the skin.

glands	bottom	sensory	dermis	vessels
waste	protective	follicles	temperature	
epidermis	millions	nerve	vitamin D	

Skin has two layers. The top is called the _____. The very top layer of cells is dead. Dead cells fall off by the _____ every day. New cells move up from the _____ of the epidermis. The layer underneath is called the _____. In the dermis, you will find blood _____, _____ endings, oil and sweat _____, and hair _____.

Your skin performs several functions. It forms a _____ covering over your body. It serves as a _____ organ, which allows you to feel things. It helps regulate the body's _____ and also participates in the production of _____. Last of all, your skin helps rid your body of _____ products.

The Nervous System

Far Out Fact: **Messages to the brain are transmitted at a speed of 180 mph.**

Webwise: http://faculty.washington.edu/chudler/introb.html#pns

The word **homeostasis** means the keeping of everything in balance. The nervous system has the job of maintaining homeostasis in your body. It must coordinate all of the other systems and be sure they are working correctly. What else does the nervous system do?

- It responds to stimuli in the environment around you. Anything you see, hear, smell, taste, touch, feel, or think of, the nervous system helps you understand it, respond to it, and remember it.

- It maintains your consciousness.

- It is responsible for your learning and your memory.

- It controls the automated parts of body systems, such as the beating of your heart, the movement of smooth muscles in your digestive system, your breathing, etc.

Parts of the Nervous System

Your nervous system is divided into two parts:

- The central nervous system: your brain and spinal cord

- The peripheral nervous system: all the other nerves in your body (including cranial nerves and spinal nerves)

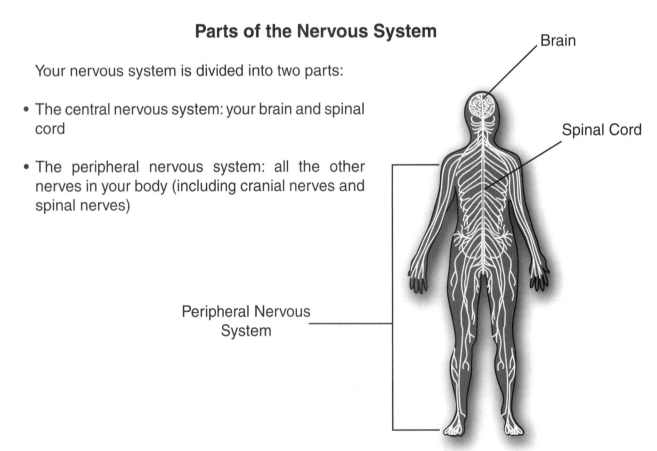

Brain

Spinal Cord

Peripheral Nervous System

Name: _____   Date: _____

A Stimulating Morning

Far Out Fact: **Your brain uses a fourth of all the body's oxygen and a fifth of all its energy supply.**

Webwise: www.innerbody.com (click on nervous system)

Think about the stimuli you encountered as you did one of these tasks this morning: got dressed, ate breakfast, traveled to school.

What did you see, hear, smell, taste, touch, feel, think about, do, remember, etc.? Your nervous system had to respond to all of these things. Write down what some of the stimuli were and how you perceived or responded to them.

Example: Eating pancakes—brain told jaw to open and close to chew; muscles automatically swallowed the chewed-up food; stomach began digestion process; nerves in nose picked up scent of pancakes and maple syrup and relayed it to brain; taste buds detected flavors of pancakes and syrup; ears heard the scraping of teeth on fork; eyes saw pancakes; hand was sent message to pick up pieces and bring to mouth; brain thought about the enjoyment of the flavors; brain remembered how to use fork to pick up pancake pieces and made decision about which piece to pick up when, etc.

_____

_____

_____

_____

_____

_____

_____

_____

_____

_____

_____

_____

_____

_____

Name: _____ Date: _____

The Brain

The human brain is divided into three parts.

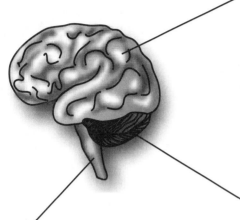

Cerebrum: This is the largest part of the brain. It is divided into two sides (called hemispheres). The outer layer is comprised of many grooves and ridges. This part of the brain is where your thinking and learning take place. It controls voluntary muscles, stores memories, and interprets sensory impulses such as vision, smell, taste, hearing, etc. The right side of the brain controls the left side of your body and is generally the creative side. The left side of the brain controls the right side of your body and generally is the logical, reasoning side.

Cerebellum: This lies behind and under the cerebrum. It helps you maintain your balance, muscle tone, and monitors voluntary muscle movements.

Brain Stem: This connects the brain to the spinal cord. It coordinates the involuntary muscle movements for functions such as the beating of your heart, your breathing, and your blood pressure.

Use your brain power to help you unscramble the sentences below and review information you have read about the brain.

1. connects brain the cord spinal The stem brain and

   _____

2. place Learning in cerebrum and take the thinking

   _____

3. muscles monitors you movements make with cerebellum The your

   _____

4. movements coordinated muscle Involuntary are the stem in brain

   _____

Neurons

Far Out Fact: The brain contains over 100 billion neurons.

Neurons are cells of the brain, spinal cord, and nerves. They look somewhat like an octopus with a long tail. Each neuron has three main parts.

Cell body: This is the main part of the cell that includes the nucleus.

Dendrites: These look like arms extending off the cell body. They receive incoming messages.

Axon: This looks like a tail extending off the cell body. It carries outgoing messages.

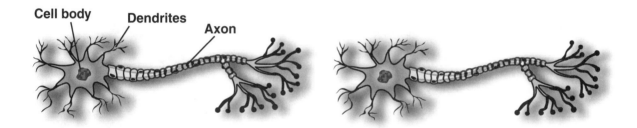

A message carried by a neuron is called an **impulse**. It travels by tiny bursts of electrical power. When an outgoing message reaches the end of the axon, the axon releases a special chemical (called a **neurotransmitter**), and the message jumps the space between neurons (called a **synapse**) and continues traveling along the dendrites of the new neuron.

Three Types of Neurons

Sensory neurons: receive information and send impulses to the spinal cord and the brain

Motor neurons: relay impulses from the brain or spinal cord to muscles and glands throughout your body

Interneurons: relay impulses between the sensory and motor neurons

Name: _____ Date: _____

Follow The Path

Far Out Fact: **The average adult brain weighs about 3 pounds.**

Use the information you learned on page 61 to help you number the following events in sequence.

_____ a. Interneurons relay the response message to motor neurons.

_____ b. Sensory neurons carry a message to your brain.

_____ c. You jump and your heart rate increases.

_____ d. Your brain determines a response.

_____ e. A balloon pops.

_____ f. The response is sent through motor neurons to your muscles.

_____ g. Sensory receptors in your ear are stimulated.

_____ h. In the brain, the response information is passed to interneurons.

The Endocrine System

Far Out Fact: Scientists are not sure what the pineal gland does.

Webwise: www.innerbody.com (click on endocrine system)

The endocrine system is another system that helps to control your body. In the nervous system, the body is controlled through messages sent along nerves. In the endocrine system, the messages are sent to tell the body what to do through the use of chemicals released into the bloodstream. These chemicals are called hormones, and each **hormone** works on different **target tissues**.

These are some of the major **glands** of the endocrine system, the hormones they release, and what they regulate.

Pituitary: This is the master gland. It releases hormones that control the other glands. It controls growth of muscles, bones, and organs with the hormone **HGH**. It also controls the reproductive glands.

Thyroid: This is a butterfly-shaped gland in the throat. It secretes the hormone **thyroxine**. This controls your body's metabolism (the rate at which your body uses up the food you eat).

Parathyroids: These four small glands regulate the levels of calcium and phosphate in your blood. They secrete **parathormone hormone**.

Adrenal glands: These sit on top of the kidneys. The outer layer makes more than 30 hormones. The inner layer makes **adrenaline**—the "fight or flight" hormone, which gives you sudden bursts of strength and energy.

Pancreas: This gland makes several hormones, including **insulin**, which helps control the blood sugar level in your body.

Name: _____ Date: _____

Endocrine Info

Use what you learned on page 63 to fill in the missing information in this chart.

Gland	Hormone Secreted	Function
		Master gland—controls other glands and growth
	Thyroxine	
Parathyroids		
		Fight or flight—sudden burst of energy and strength
Pancreas		

Explain the similarity between the endocrine system and the nervous system.

_____

_____

_____

_____

_____

Name: _____ Date: _____

Sight

Webwise: http://www.kidshealth.org/kid/htbw/eyes.html

Unscramble the names of the parts of the eye on the diagram, and then use the words from the bank to fill in the blanks in the paragraph below.

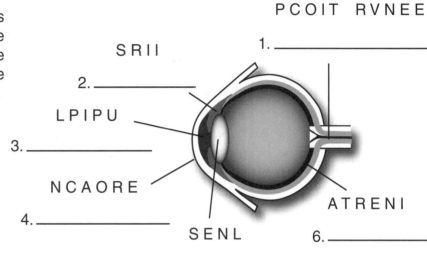

PCOIT RVNEE

1. _____

SRII

2. _____

LPIPU

3. _____

NCAORE

4. _____

SENL

5. _____

ATRENI

6. _____

rods	back	cones	optic nerve
cornea	brain	sensitive	bright
lens	colors	dim	retina

Light waves enter your eyes and are bent first by the _____,

followed by the _____. The rays of light are then directed onto the

_____, which sits at the very _____ of

your eye. This tissue is extremely _____ to light energy and contains

two kinds of cells called _____ and _____.

Rods respond to _____ light, while cones respond to

_____ lights and _____. The

energy from the light waves stimulates impulses in the rods and cones. These impulses

travel to the _____, which carries them to the

_____ where the image is interpreted.

Name: _____ Date: _____

Hearing

Webwise: http://www.kidshealth.org/kid/htbw/ears.html

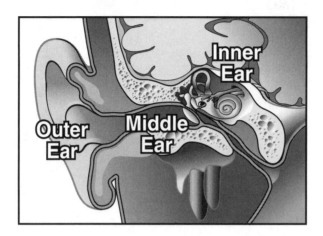

Number these steps in order to describe how you come to hear the sound of a plucked guitar string.

_____ a. The vibrating air travels in a wave-like pattern to your ear.

_____ b. The stirrup bone taps against a membrane on the opening to the inner ear, which causes the cochlea to vibrate.

_____ c. The guitar string is plucked, causing it to vibrate.

_____ d. The sound waves cause the eardrum to vibrate at the same speed.

_____ e. As it vibrates, nerve endings in the cochlea are stimulated, sending nerve impulses along the auditory nerve to the brain.

_____ f. The vibration of the string causes air particles surrounding it to begin vibrating also.

_____ g. The vibrations from the eardrum travel through three small bones: the hammer, the anvil, and the stirrup.

_____ h. The outer ear canal traps the sound waves and funnels them down the canal to your eardrum.

_____ i. The brain interprets the impulses to determine the type of sound.